INVERCLYDE EDUCATION RESOURCE SERVICE

Performance Management

for School Improvement

This book is due for return on or before the last date shown below.

Performance Management
for School Improvement

A Practical Guide for Secondary Schools

Jeff Jones

David Fulton Publishers
London

David Fulton Publishers Ltd
Ormond House, 26–27 Boswell Street, London WC1N 3JZ

www.fultonpublishers.co.uk

First published in Great Britain by David Fulton Publishers 2001

Note: The right of Jeff Jones to be identified as the author of this work has been asserted by him in accordance with the Copyright, Designs and Patents Act 1988.

British Library Cataloguing in Publication Data
A catalogue record for this book is available from the British Library.

ISBN 1–85346–769-3

Note:
On the back cover of the book the author is described as Senior Education Advisor for the Council of British Teachers. This should read *The Centre for British Teachers* (*CfBT*). The publishers apologise for this error.

Typeset by Book Production Services, London
Printed in Great Britain by Bell & Bain Ltd, Glasgow

Contents

Acknowledgements

The author wishes to acknowledge the support and contribution of colleagues from schools, LEAs and consultancies, as well as at the DfEE, in the writing of this book.

Introduction

There appears to be no discernible reduction in the level of challenge being laid before any of us involved in the work of schools to find ways of raising the achievement of pupils. If anything, the demand for improvement and higher standards in schools is intensifying and the level of new initiatives aimed at their achievement is escalating. Given that effective teachers continue to be key determinants of successful pupil learning, it is understandable that some of the current initiatives, emanating centrally, are firmly focused on managing teachers' performance and on supporting them in their professional development. The recent introduction of performance management is one such initiative.

Although performance management has been an influential development in human resource management since the mid-1980s, the concept is comparatively new to schools and to the teaching profession. Advocates of the new performance management arrangements within the sphere of education, chiefly the Department for Education and Employment (DfEE), will wish schools to gain from the continuous and integrated approach to managing and rewarding performance that has already led to benefits in other public-sector and commercial organisations.

The performance management system being introduced by the DfEE has arisen in large measure from the already established but somewhat discredited statutory appraisal system set up in the early 1990s. It is not the intention here to contemplate the reasons for the demise of appraisal, but simply to remind readers that the earlier arrangements failed to deliver the results that the profession had sought, namely improvements in pupil standards and in the quality of teaching and learning.

Performance management, which came into statutory force in September 2000 for schools in England, offers a strategic and integrated process with the potential to deliver sustained improvements in schools by improving the performance of teachers generally and by developing their capacity as members of teams and as individual contributors.

This book has been written with secondary schools specifically in mind in order to take account of their unique circumstances as they attempt to introduce performance management with rigour, yet with sensitivity. It is a book that offers a set of general guidelines on strategic elements of the process as well as the all-important operational ones. The book offers a set of principles for effective practice, which if used with vigilance and tailored appropriately for schools' particular organisational needs should help ensure a rational and valuable performance management process. With this in mind, the book is organised in a straightforward and, hopefully, accessible way.

Chapter 1 highlights the ways in which performance management can assist schools to improve and the benefits likely to accrue for teachers and their pupils. It describes the framework within which teachers and their team leaders agree and review objectives set within the school's own priorities for development. The performance management cycle and the respective roles of school personnel in the process are also set out.

In Chapter 2, the planning stage of the performance management cycle is described and guidance is offered on the role of self-review in helping to focus the review and identify priorities. The chapter also focuses on how objectives are agreed, what categories they should cover and the criteria for their construction.

The monitoring stage of the cycle is the theme of Chapter 3. Guidance is offered on methods for tracking the progress of objectives, including the role of lesson observation. Attention is also given to the form that supportive action might take in helping teachers to fulfil their commitment to professional development, as set out in their personal development plans.

Chapter 4 looks at the performance review stage of the cycle – how to maximise the opportunity this offers team leaders and teachers to reflect on performance in a structured way and to identify areas for improvement and further development.

The final chapter provides a monitoring and evaluation framework for use by schools when gauging the effectiveness of its arrangements. The framework is made up of a series of individual evaluation schedules that can be used in their entirety or one focus area at a time.

Chapter 1

Performance management

In September 2000 the Department for Education and Employment (DfEE) introduced a statutory system of performance management for all teachers and head teachers in England. The Education (School Teacher Appraisal) (England) Regulations 2000[1] replaced the earlier appraisal regulations (DES 1991) and have required schools to review their existing arrangements for monitoring and appraisal and to agree a new performance management policy.

The intention behind the introduction of performance management is for schools to demonstrate commitment to:

> develop all teachers effectively to ensure job satisfaction, high levels of expertise and progression of staff in their chosen profession.
>
> (*Performance Management in Schools*, DfEE April 2000a: 1)

The Government's belief is that where schools and teachers have clear expectations about what pupils should achieve, there is a greater likelihood that standards will rise. The Government views performance management as a means of assisting schools by supporting teachers in their work and helping them improve their skills and capabilities. This is why it has made performance management such a key feature of its Green Paper proposals.

The Green Paper

The Government's Green Paper *Teachers: Meeting the Challenge of Change* (DfEE 1998) proposed an interlocking set of reforms to strengthen the teaching profession through:

- better leadership;
- better rewards;

Background

- better training; and
- better support.

One of the central proposals was that performance management should help to:

- develop a stronger link between teachers' work and the school's development plan;
- encourage regular and more meaningful discussion between teachers and those colleagues who were best acquainted with their work; and
- provide a framework within which teachers could consider their career and professional development.

Performance management, introduced with sensitivity and managed effectively, supports teachers in meeting the needs of pupils and in raising standards. According to the DfEE, there are two major beneficiaries of performance management:

PUPILS	TEACHERS
... because their teachers will have a better idea of what their pupils can achieve with the right kind of support and encouragement.	... because their performance will be judged on a regular and systematic basis and there will be opportunities for them to discuss their work and development with their team leaders.

However, there are also benefits for the school as a whole. Performance management has the potential to:

- add clarification to the school's aims and objectives;
- coordinate teachers' development priorities with those of the school and its subject areas;
- contribute an injection of energy into the school through the formulation of improvement objectives;
- bring about a closer match between individuals' capabilities and the school's role specifications;
- ensure greater clarity regarding staff responsibilities;
- encourage team building and a wider exchange of ideas;
- encourage more effective communication;
- enhance school ethos; and
- promote better focused professional development opportunities.

To be effective, performance management should be set in the context of other complementary management processes that exist within the school, i.e. integrated into the way the school is managed and linked with other key processes. Figure 1.1 illustrates some of the key integration opportunities.

Integration of performance management with complementary processes

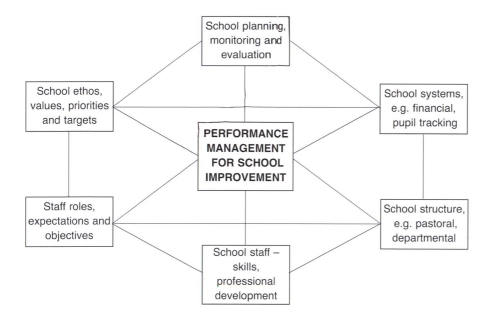

Figure 1.1: Integration of performance management with other key processes

It makes little sense for performance management to proceed without close reference to the school's plans for development, which themselves should be set against the background of the LEA's Education Development Plan, other local initiatives such as Excellence in Cities, national priorities and recommendations made following OFSTED inspection. Successful integration involves aligning:

- the school's strategic plans and goals with individual and team objectives;
- the values and capabilities of the school with the values and capabilities achieved by individual teachers; and
- other performance management strategies with other 'people' strategies, such as valuing, rewarding and developing.

Performance management policy

The DfEE requires schools to have an agreed, written performance management policy. Such a policy is intended to ensure that members of the school community understand:

- what performance management is intended to achieve;
- how performance management works within their school; and
- what their responsibilities and rights are within the process.

> The policy should be fair, treat all teachers consistently and be simple to operate and implement... The policy should encourage teachers to share good practice and build upon a shared understanding of teaching skills.
> (*Performance Management in Schools*, DfEE April 2000a: 4)

Minimally, the school's policy should set out its:

- *commitment* to agree, monitor and review objectives with every teacher;
- *annual timetable* clearly linked to the school planning cycle and arrangements to monitor progress and improvement; and
- *standard documentation* for use by all teachers at the school.

The DfEE has provided schools with a model policy (DfEE 2000) designed to help them apply the regulations rigorously and consistently. The DfEE's model policy contains elements that are strongly recommended (R) and others that are statutory (S) and therefore must be included without amendment. Figure 1.2 provides schools with an audit framework for gauging the extent to which their own performance management policy meets the requirements of the DfEE model:

POLICY SECTION	SCOPE AND CONTENT OF SECTION	R	S
1. INTRODUCTION	Introduces the contents of the policy and locates it in the new performance management system which has statutory effect from 1 September 2000.	✔	
2. RATIONALE	Explains the school's vision for performance management. It sets out some of the benefits of performance management, as described in the DfEE's framework.	✔	
3. ROLES	Introduces the roles and responsibilities of different staff in the performance management process. Each school will need to be clear about roles and responsibilities under the performance management system. In this policy document the term 'team leader' refers to a teacher who, on the basis of responsibility for learning in the school, has the best overview of the teacher's work and the ability to provide support to staff. The team leader is the person who will carry out the review.	✔	
4. RESPONSIBILITY FOR REVIEWS	Shows how the school plans its reviews so that each teacher understands who is responsible for his or her performance review. For example, the head may be the team leader for all school staff in a small school or team leader of the senior management team in a larger school. Where a team is too large for the leader to be the reviewer for all the team, the task could be shared with others who hold significant management posts within the team. Schools should consider the time involved in doing a number of performance management reviews.	✔	
5. TIMING OF REVIEWS	Clarifies the timing of the school's review cycle and takes account of the statutory requirements for setting objectives and the length of the review cycle. The review cycle operates on a continuous one-year cycle, except for the first year, when schools have the option of setting a cycle of between 9 and 18 months for teachers only. The Regulations specify that the governing body decides on the timing for the head's review cycle and the head decides on the timing for teachers' reviews. The head needs to consider the workload implications and how the cycle will fit best with the school's other planning arrangements. After the first cycle, planning should flow naturally from the previous year's review.	✔	✔
6. PERFORMANCE MANAGEMENT CYCLE	Explains the cycle of planning, monitoring and reviewing performance as it will operate in the school. The governing body is responsible for performance review and for agreeing the performance management policy. The head is responsible for	✔	✔

Figure 1.2: Performance management policy audit framework

POLICY SECTION	SCOPE AND CONTENT OF SECTION	R	S
	implementing the policy. The circumstances in which teachers work and the range of responsibilities they carry out vary considerably. Discussions should be set in the context of the professional duties set out in the School Teachers' Pay and Conditions document and the teacher's own work and job description.		
7. LINKS BETWEEN PAY, CAREER STAGES AND PERFORMANCE MANAGEMENT	Sets out the links between the performance management systems and other policies and how the performance management process may impact on them. Schools may want to expand this section to include more details on other school policies, such as professional development. Schools should explain either here or in the school's pay policy how information from reviews will be used to inform decisions on teachers' pay for all those who are eligible for performance pay points.	✔	✔
8. MANAGING WEAK PERFORMANCE	Clarifies the position of performance management in any case of staff under-performance	✔	✔
9. CONFIDENTIALITY	Sets out the confidential nature of performance management.	✔	
10. ACCESS TO OUTCOMES	Shows the statutory position regarding access to review statements or information contained within them.	✔	✔
11. COMPLAINTS	Details the process to follow if a complaint is made about the review process This section explains the procedures for complaining about reviews.		✔
12 EVALUATION OF THE POLICY	Confirms the importance of ongoing evaluation of the review process.	✔	✔
13. STANDARDISED DOCUMENTATION	Includes the documentation to be used in association with the process.	✔	

Figure 1.2: Performance management policy audit framework (continued)

The length of the DfEE's performance review cycle is intended to be one year, although head teachers are permitted to reduce this to 9 months or extend it to 18 months in the first year of operation. Some schools will value this flexibility so that they can accommodate other managerial procedures, take account of the impact of a host of other initiatives and urgent contextual factors, e.g. OFSTED inspection, and incorporate performance review arrangements into school development and target-setting processes.

The annual cycle need not follow the school year, the calendar year or indeed the financial year. It is up to schools to discuss and agree the precise timing of the cycle. Most are basing this decision on the availability of their development plan priorities and appropriate pupil progress data, e.g. PANDA, target-setting data. Ongoing in its nature, the performance management cycle comprises three stages (Figure 1.3 and Figure 1.4).

The performance management cycle

STAGE 1	PLANNING:	Team leaders discuss and record priorities and objectives with each of the teachers in their team. They discuss how progress will be monitored.
STAGE 2	MONITORING:	The teacher and team leader keep progress under review throughout the cycle, taking any supportive action needed.
STAGE 3	REVIEW:	The teacher and the team leader review achievements over the year and evaluate the teacher's overall performance, taking account of progress against objectives.

Figure 1.3: The stages of the performance management cycle

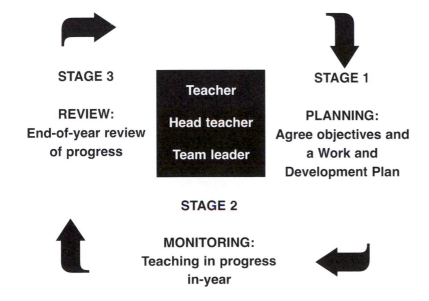

Figure 1.4: The performance management cycle

Roles and responsibilities

Implementing the performance management system will require clear definition of roles and responsibilities for key players in the process. A prominent role is that of team leader which in the DfEE guidance refers to:

> ... a teacher who has the best overview of the teacher's work and is able to support staff. The team leader is normally the person who will carry out the review.
> (*Performance Management Framework*, DfEE April 2000a: 3)

This is an attempt to acknowledge the fact that, in large measure, teachers contribute as members of teams, e.g. subject, pastoral, key stage. Whereas the team leader of staff in a small primary school may well be the head teacher, in secondary schools, the role of team leader is likely to be undertaken by subject leaders, key stage coordinators or members of the senior management team or leadership group. Sheer weight of numbers in some areas of the school may necessitate a sharing of the team leader role with others in the area, e.g. second in the department.

Figure 1.5 offers a summary of the major responsibilities that key personnel will be required to undertake in the implementation of performance management.

Role	Summary of responsibilities
Governing body	• is responsible for agreeing the school's performance management policy, for ensuring that teachers' performance is regularly and systematically reviewed, and for monitoring the overall process; • does not have a role in gathering evidence or in making judgements about individual teachers; • has a duty to review the head teacher's performance, with the support of an approved external adviser; • should decide on the exact timing of the head teacher's performance review cycle and appoint two to three governors to carry out the review.
Chair of Governors	• is the review officer for complaints from the head teacher where s/he has not played a part in the actual review;

Figure 1.5: Roles and responsibilities of personnel in performance management

Role	Summary of responsibilities
	• provides any review officer or new reviewer with a copy of the review statement and with the objectives relating to that statement; • passes the training and development annex of the head teacher's review statement to the person responsible for training and development in the school; • provides a summary of the overall assessment of performance section of the head teacher's review statement to the chief education officer, or representative, on request; • provides a copy of the head teacher's appraisal statement to the chief education officer, or a designated officer, where the school does not have a delegated budget.
Governors responsible for the head teacher's review	• must seek advice from the appointed external adviser when setting objectives and reviewing the performance of the head teacher; • meet with the head teacher and adviser at the start of the review cycle to plan and prepare for the performance review, and set and record head teacher objectives relating to school leadership and management and pupil progress; • meet with the head teacher and external adviser at the end of the review cycle to review the head teacher's performance and to identify achievements, including assessment of achievement against objectives, and to discuss and identify professional development needs/activities; • write a performance review statement and give a copy to the head teacher within ten working days of the review meeting, and allow a further ten working days for the head teacher to add written comments; • provide the head teacher and chair of governors with a copy of the head teacher's review statement; • on request, provide a copy of the head teacher's statement to those governors who are responsible for taking decisions in relation to promotion and pay; and they should take account of this when making such decisions.

Figure 1.5: Roles and responsibilities of personnel in performance management (continued)

Role	Summary of responsibilities
Head teacher	• is responsible for the overall implementation of the school's performance management policy and for ensuring that the performance management reviews take place; • is responsible for appointing team leaders for each teacher to carry out the performance review and for deciding on the exact timing of those reviews; • will need to take account of teachers' performance reviews in making recommendations to the governing body about teachers' pay; • reviews complaints by teachers about their performance review statement; • provides an annual report on performance management for consideration by the governing body; • keeps teachers' review statements on file and provides access to information from these statements as outlined in the Regulations.
Team leader	The team leader must: • meet with each of the teachers for whom they are the reviewer before or at the start of the performance review cycle to plan and prepare for performance review and discuss setting objectives; • record objectives in writing and allow the job holder to add written comments if they wish; • monitor performance against these objectives throughout the year and observe the teacher teaching in the classroom at least once during the review cycle; • consult the reviewee before obtaining oral or written information from others relating to the teacher's performance; • meet with the teacher at the end of the review cycle to review performance and identify achievements, including assessment of achievement against objectives, and to discuss and identify professional development needs/activities; • write a performance review statement and give a copy to the reviewee within ten working days of the final review meeting and allow a further ten working days for the job holder to add written comments;

Figure 1.5: Roles and responsibilities of personnel in performance management (continued)

Role	Summary of responsibilities
	• pass the completed review statement to the head teacher.
Teachers	• must meet with their team leader before or at the start of the performance review cycle to discuss setting objectives; • either agree objectives with the team leader or add written comments to the objectives recorded by the team leader; • must meet with their team leader at the end of the review cycle to review performance and identify achievement, including assessment of achievement against objectives, and to discuss and identify professional development needs/activities; • may add comments to the review statement or complain about their review statement within ten working days of receipt from the team leader.

Figure 1.5: Roles and responsibilities of personnel in performance management (continued)

In their implementation of performance management, schools should attempt to build on the good practice that already exists. Schools are unlikely to have to start afresh when developing their policy because the majority will already have a clear and coordinated policy for appraisal and staff development that supports individual staff as well as overall school needs, e.g. Investors in People. Where this is the case, schools will use this platform to establish their modified arrangements for performance management.

Reviewing existing arrangements

For some schools, it will be a 'cultural' platform, such as the existence of high levels of trust and openness among colleagues that encourages them to share the strengths and the weaknesses of their practice without fear. In other schools, visits by peers and team leaders to classrooms to observe lessons will be willingly accepted and encouraged. In others, this process will be reciprocated, leading to a two-way traffic of information and sharing. Other cultural platforms found in schools include:

- shared goals;
- collegiality;
- shared commitment to continuous improvement;
- risk taking and risk sharing;
- joint celebration;

11

- humour;
- team approaches; and
- open feedback.

In the case of schools that have achieved or are working towards the Investors in People, the rationale underpinning performance management will pose few difficulties.

Another kind of platform upon which schools can establish their performance management arrangements is the 'systems' platform. In schools where systems are supportive and well conceived, planning, monitoring and review are already an integral part of their approach towards development planning, performance data management, pupil target setting and professional development.

However, schools will find themselves at various stages of awareness and development in respect of performance management and consequently may find the following schedule (Figure 1.6) of help should they decide to audit the existing arrangements for monitoring and appraisal. The audit schedule which takes account of the 'Key Steps in Performance Management' found in Annex A of the DfEE's *Performance Mangement Framework* (April 2000a: 10, 11), poses relevant prompting questions and suggests the evidence base within which responses might be located.

KEY QUESTIONS FOR SCHOOLS	EVIDENCE SOURCE
MAKING A COMMITMENT	
How does the school demonstrate its commitment to the performance management process?	Policy documentation Discussion with HT/SMT Sample staff views
Has the school taken account of the new arrangements in agreeing its performance management policy?	Policy documentation Discussion with HT/SMT Sample staff views
Was the policy ready for implementation in September 2000?	Policy documentation Discussion with HT/SMT Sample staff views

Figure 1.6: Auditing the school's existing arrangements

KEY QUESTIONS FOR SCHOOLS	EVIDENCE SOURCE
How were staff involved in the formulation of the policy?	Policy documentation Discussion with HT/SMT Sample staff views
How effectively does the policy set out the rationale and purpose of performance management?	Policy documentation Discussion with HT/SMT Sample staff views
How effectively does the policy integrate with the school's development planning processes?	Policy documentation Discussion with HT/SMT Sample staff views
What steps have been taken to ensure that the process is carried out in a fair and consistent manner?	Policy documentation Discussion with HT/SMT Sample staff views
How does the senior management team model the type of performance management it wishes teachers to demonstrate?	Policy documentation Discussion with HT/SMT Observation of SMT practices Sample staff views Staff development records
Does the school have a vision and/or mission statement?	Policy documentation Vision/mission statement Sample staff views
DEFINING ROLES	
Who is responsible for the development and implementation of the performance management policy?	Policy documentation Discussion with HT/SMT Sample staff views
Who has responsibility for individuals' performance review?	Policy documentation Discussion with HT/SMT Sample staff views
Do all teaching staff have job descriptions that accurately reflect their roles and responsibilities?	Policy documentation Job descriptions Sample staff views

Figure 1.6: Auditing the school's existing arrangements (continued)

KEY QUESTIONS FOR SCHOOLS	EVIDENCE SOURCE
Do all support staff have job descriptions that accurately reflect their roles and responsibilities?	Policy documentation Job descriptions Sample staff views
AGREEING RESPONSIBILITIES AND TIMETABLE	
Has the nature, extent and timing of teachers' involvement been clearly set out?	Policy documentation Discussion with HT/SMT Sample staff views
Has the timetable been linked with the school's planning cycle and existing monitoring arrangements?	Policy documentation Discussion with HT/SMT Sample staff views
AGREEING POLICY AND DOCUMENTATION	
Have all teachers been issued with the relevant documentation?	Policy documentation Discussion with HT/SMT Sample staff views
Are the forms understood and used consistently?	Discussion with HT/SMT Sample staff views
PLANNING AND SETTING OBJECTIVES	
Do all staff have explicit termly or annual job targets?	Discussion with HT/SMT Sample staff views
Do the targets cover pupil progress and ways of developing the teacher's effectiveness?	Discussion with HT/SMT Sample staff views
How are staff helped with their planning to meet objectives?	Policy documentation Discussion with HT/SMT Sample staff views
What guidance is available to staff on other school processes which will need to be considered in formulating individual objectives?	Policy documentation Discussion with HT/SMT Sample staff views

Figure 1.6: Auditing the school's existing arrangements (continued)

KEY QUESTIONS FOR SCHOOLS	EVIDENCE SOURCE
How do professional development objectives relate to the school's overall priorities for staff development, including the use of funding for INSET?	Policy documentation Discussion with HT/SMT Sample staff views
MONITORING PROGRESS	
How effective are the arrangements for monitoring in-year to ensure that both team leaders and teachers gather enough information to discuss overall performance?	Policy documentation Discussion with HT/SMT Sample staff views
How clear are the criteria for handling classroom observation, the guidelines about feedback and the way in which it fits into review arrangements?	Policy documentation Discussion with HT/SMT Sample staff views
How actively involved are teachers in their performance review?	Policy documentation Discussion with HT/SMT Sample staff views
PERFORMANCE REVIEW	
Are all staff involved in a professional review or appraisal process?	Policy documentation Discussion with HT/SMT Sample staff views
Are teachers afforded proper opportunities to discuss their work and their professional development with their team leader?	Policy documentation Sample staff views
How frequently is their performance assessed?	Policy documentation Discussion with HT/SMT Sample staff views
How are staff helped to prepare for the annual review meeting, e.g. self-appraisal?	Policy documentation Discussion with HT/SMT Sample staff views
What steps are taken to structure discussion to cover specific objectives, general discussion of strengths and achievements and agreement on strategies to develop skills or techniques?	Policy documentation Discussion with HT/SMT Sample staff views
How well are the outcomes of performance reviews used to set priorities for teachers' professional development?	Policy documentation Discussion with HT/SMT Sample staff views

Figure 1.6: Auditing the school's existing arrangements (continued)

KEY QUESTIONS FOR SCHOOLS	EVIDENCE SOURCE
How effectively are review outcomes used by the governing body to make decisions about discretionary pay awards?	Policy documentation Discussion with HT/SMT Governor representative
STAFF DEVELOPMENT PROGRAMME	
How well does the staff development programme take account of whole-school, team and individual needs?	Policy documentation Staff development programme Discussion with HT/SMT Sample staff views Evaluations
How is the programme costed in terms of time and money?	Policy documentation Discussion with HT/SMT
How does the school evaluate the impact of the programme?	Policy documentation Staff development programme Discussion with HT/SMT Sample staff views
GOVERNORS	
How effectively does the governing body perform its strategic role in respect of the school's performance management policy?	Policy documentation Discussion with HT/SMT Governor representative
How effectively does the governing body meet its responsibilities for setting objectives and reviewing the performance of heads, deputies and ASTs for pay purposes?	Policy documentation Discussion with HT/SMT Governor representative
PERFORMANCE REVIEW INFORMATION	
How does the school ensure that each teacher receives a copy of his/her review and work and development form?	Policy documentation Discussion with HT/SMT Sample staff views
How does the school ensure that the head receives copies of all review statements?	Policy documentation Discussion with HT/SMT

Figure 1.6: Auditing the school's existing arrangements (continued)

KEY QUESTIONS FOR SCHOOLS	EVIDENCE SOURCE
How does the teacher responsible for planning and development receive information about professional development needs?	Policy documentation Discussion with HT/SMT Sample staff views
What mechanism exists for the head to report on performance management to designated governors?	Policy documentation Discussion with HT/SMT
How does the school ensure that a summary of the reviews is given to the governing body?	Policy documentation Discussion with HT/SMT
What arrangements exist for ensuring that a copy of the head's statement is forwarded to the LEA?	Policy documentation Discussion with HT/SMT
LINKING REVIEWS TO PAY AND OTHER POLICIES	
In what ways have the links between pay and career stages and performance management been explained to staff and governors?	Policy documentation Discussion with HT/SMT
What arrangement exists for ensuring that reviews are linked to significant career points, e.g. induction?	Policy documentation Discussion with HT/SMT
How will performance review be used to inform considerations about threshold?	Policy documentation Discussion with HT/SMT
How will performance review be used to inform considerations about performance pay points above the threshold?	Policy documentation Discussion with HT/SMT
MONITORING AND EVALUATION	
How does the school ensure that the policy is updated and improved over time?	Policy documentation Discussion with HT/SMT
TRAINING	
How will the audit of training needs be conducted?	Policy documentation Discussion with HT/SMT
What arrangements have been put in place to provide appropriate INSET for staff ?	Policy documentation Discussion with HT/SMT

Figure 1.6: Auditing the school's existing arrangements (continued)

KEY QUESTIONS FOR SCHOOLS	EVIDENCE SOURCE
How have the two additional training days been used to support the school's arrangements for performance management?	Policy documentation Discussion with HT/SMT
APPEALS PROCEDURES AND CONFIDENTIALITY	
Are staff aware of the appeals procedure?	Policy documentation Discussion with HT/SMT Sample staff views
Are there rules of confidentiality in place?	Policy documentation Discussion with HT/SMT Sample staff views

Ethical considerations

To achieve its goals effectively, performance management should operate in accordance with certain ethical principles:

Fairness

All individuals within the organisation should be treated in a similar fashion when they are being reviewed. This does not mean that they must all receive the same type of review, but it does mean that the same guidelines are used for designing the review, carrying it out, and reaching conclusions and judgements about performance. If the data used in the review is objective and gathered properly and the review itself is well planned, then the outcome is more likely to be fair.

Equality

A sense of equality between the reviewer and the reviewee is important. The reviewer will usually be senior to the reviewee but that should not mean a sense of equality cannot be engendered. Both parties need to be able to talk freely and to exchange ideas without fear of rebuke.

Note

1. Readers should refer to these Regulations for details of all mandatory requirements associated with performance management.

Chapter 2

The performance management cycle: planning stage

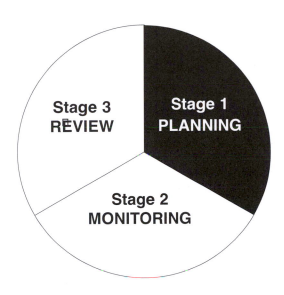

Planning, the first stage in the performance management cycle, invites each teacher to discuss and agree objectives with his/her team leader and to record these in an individual plan. A process of self-review can be of tremendous help to teachers preparing for this stage of the performance management process.

As part of their preparation for the performance review, teachers should be encouraged to recognise the value of self-review and to carry it out. Self-review, though not compulsory, has the potential to inform all other aspects of the performance review process and thus help teachers gain maximum benefit from it. Self-review may be useful at various stages in the performance review cycle but it is likely to be of greatest value:

- prior to the planning meeting (Stage 1) to help identify a focus and clarify objectives;
- as preparation for lesson observation (Stage 2);
- during/following lesson observation (Stage 2); and
- as preparation for the review meeting (Stage 3).

Self-review

Specifically, teacher self-review can help:

- ensure that performance management is a two-way process;
- ensure that the teacher clarifies his/her thoughts and knows what s/he wants to gain from the process;
- encourage ongoing reflection in order to celebrate success and establish strategies for improvement.

To be effective, self-review should:

- prompt reflection on the teacher's work in a structured way;
- cover appropriate aspects of the teacher's job;
- include a view of how the job should be done;
- give rise to reliable data to underpin objective setting;
- establish a clear picture of the teacher's performance;
- not take up a disproportionate amount of time;
- provide information which leads to improvement in the quality of teaching and learning and to raised standards; and
- accommodate the school's improvement philosophy.

Self-review may be recorded in various ways, ranging from formal, structured means to ones that are rather more spontaneous. The important requirement is that the recording mechanism assists the process of reflection. As with all performance review documents – prompt sheets and pro formas – they need to be considered carefully before they are adopted. Discussions will need to take place in order to reach agreement about the confidentiality aspects surrounding self-appraisal, for example:

- Are the completed pro formas intended for the reviewee's use only?
- Should sharing of the contents of a self-review pro forma be left to the reviewee alone?
- Should the self-review be shared with the team leader prior to any discussion?

Above all, self-review pro formas should suit the context of the school and be consistent with the school's approach to performance management. The development of a school self-review form can be an activity that encourages staff to consider the value of self-review. In an attempt to facilitate discussion among staff about a workable format, examples of self-review forms are set out below.

EXAMPLE 1: SELF-APPRAISAL FORMAT

1. Which aspects of your job do you enjoy and why?

2. Which parts of your job do you like least and why?

3. Do you have skills or abilities that you do not use in your job? Which ones?

4. Under what conditions do you work most effectively?

5.　Which are your key job skills?

6.　What other skills or knowledge do you feel would be useful to you currently?

7.　Are there any key training needs that emerge from your agreed objectives?

8.　What additional training or experience do you think you need at this stage?

EXAMPLE 2: SELF-APPRAISAL FORMAT

1.   JOB DESCRIPTION

Set down a brief list of what you consider to be the key tasks and responsibilities of your job.

2.   THE YEAR'S WORK

What have you done with greatest satisfaction?

How could these aspects of your work be used to best advantage?

What have you done with least satisfaction?

What could be done to overcome these difficulties?

3.   OBSTACLES

Were there any obstacles which hindered you in accomplishing what you wished?

Are they likely to recur?

If so, how could they be eliminated?

4. **IMPROVEMENT**
   To make your job performance better, what additional things might be done by:

   a) your head teacher?

   b) yourself?

   c) team leader?

   d) anyone else?

5. **TARGETS FOR NEXT YEAR**
   What do you think should be the key aims in your targets for next year?

6. **CAREER PROGRESSION**
   Do you have any plans for career development?

EXAMPLE 3: SELF-APPRAISAL FORMAT

1.   What do you consider to be the main tasks and responsibilities of your current post?

2.   During the past academic year, what aspects of your work have given you:

   a) the greatest satisfaction?

   b) the least satisfaction?

3.   Did anything prevent you from achieving something you had intended or hoped to do?

4.   Have these obstacles been removed?

5. What in your view would be the main goals for the next year?

6. What help do you need to this end and from whom?

7. How do you envisage your career developing?

EXAMPLE 4: SELF-APPRAISAL FORMAT					
		High		Low	
How do I rate my:	1	2	3	4	5
Organisation of work within my areas of responsibility?					
Ability to lead colleagues, drawing together their ideas and developing good practice?					
Ability to support, influence and develop the work of colleagues for whom I am responsible?					
Work in liaising with colleagues in complementary roles in feeder and transfer schools?					
Effectiveness in maintaining records for which I am responsible?					
Work in liaising with teachers in related areas of responsibility?					
Consideration of recent reports and developments in the areas for which I am responsible?					
Effectiveness in keeping others informed about the work in my areas of responsibility?					
Skills in counselling colleagues who need my help?					
Skill in running meetings?					

EXAMPLE 5: SELF-APPRAISAL FORMAT

Making reference to your job description consider the following elements of your work.

CURRICULUM – OTHER RESPONSIBILITIES

1. With which aspects of your job and work do you feel especially pleased?

2. Which aspects of your job have not gone as well as you had hoped?

3. Are you working under any constraints or difficulties?

TEACHING RESPONSIBILITIES

4. Are you happy with the age group you are teaching?

5. Read through the analysis of teaching schedule. In which area do you feel your strengths lie?

6. Choose two different areas of pupil progress which you feel would benefit from further analysis. Decide what information/data you would like collected by your reviewer which would throw light on these areas.

STAFF DEVELOPMENT PORTFOLIO

7. Identify any achievements you would like added to your portfolio.

8. List all INSET/courses attended – qualifications gained in the last year.

9. What are your objectives next year with regard to your curriculum and other responsibilities?

10. Are there any ways in which you would like to develop your experience and strengthen your expertise in the coming year?

EXAMPLE 6: SELF-APPRAISAL FORMAT
AREAS FOR DISCUSSION:
JOB DESCRIPTION: Are you clear about what it states?   Are there any amendments you wish to make?
AREAS OF SUCCESS: Which aspect/areas of your role have pleased you this year?
DIFFICULTIES THAT HAVE OCCURRED: What difficulties have arisen and what assistance might you need with respect to these?
AREAS FOR DEVELOPMENT: Which areas of your role do you particularly wish to develop?
OBJECTIVES/TARGETS: What objectives do you wish to achieve this year?
SUPPORT: Is there any support you would welcome in either professional or personal development terms?

Effective self-review can help identify the teacher's priorities for the forthcoming 12–month period. The discussion between the team leader and the teacher regarding perceived priorities is an important and substantial aspect of the planning process. It is highly likely that the priorities stem from a combination of sources; among them are the following:

Discussing priorities and setting objectives

- teachers' own views of their practice and understanding of their role;
- team leaders' perceptions of teachers' roles and present levels of success in fulfilling such roles;
- the priorities identified via school development and area plans;
- the priorities set by OFSTED following inspection;
- the requirements of examination boards/assessment authorities;
- the requirements of government agencies, e.g. QCA;
- feedback on practice provided internally through monitoring procedures and/or externally through reviews undertaken by the LEA, for example.

Priorities identified in these ways form the basis of the discussion and eventual agreement that needs to take place between team leader and teachers regarding objective setting. To a greater or lesser extent, performance management is about managing expectations. These expectations are defined in the form of objectives which are finite, time-related and person-specific. Put simply, objectives describe priorities that have to be accomplished – a goal, objective or course of action that might be appropriate for the teacher to aim for. Objective setting cannot take place in isolation. Ideally, the objectives should harmonise with the broader priorities identified following the school development planning process. In this way the involvement of staff is encouraged through their identification of individual professional needs and their contribution to wider development planning.

The intention, then, is that teachers' objectives should emerge from discussions between team leaders and teachers about priorities for the forthcoming 12 months. Specifically, the discussion should centre on particular ways in which the teacher can assist his/her pupils to improve. Such discussions could focus on the steps that might be taken to target the progress of a small number of pupils whose lack of improvement is of concern. Alternatively, the objective setting might focus on the teacher's wish or need to develop new skills or techniques for use in the classroom, e.g. acquiring the skills of open questioning, more effective resources management, more effective group work, etc.

There is no golden rule about how many objectives there should be for teachers. Objectives should be determined within the context in which individual teachers operate and in accordance with their developmental needs and those of their pupils. Generally, the objectives set at the planning meeting should be two to five in number and relate to categories identified by the DfEE (Figure 2.1).

> Teacher objectives will cover pupil progress as well as ways of developing and improving teachers' professional practice. The head's objectives will cover school leadership and management as well as pupil progress.
>
> (*Model Performance Management Policy*, DfEE 2000b: 4)

1. Professional development	Professional development objectives would support teachers in acquiring skills in order to develop their work in the classroom. They might include observation of other colleagues at work within their own or in another curriculum area/school, attending INSET courses.
2. Pupil progress	Schools will make use of what is known about pupils to help determine objectives within this category. Internal and external assessments, PANDAs and bench-marking data can each make valuable contributions to discussion.
3. Leadership and management	Where teachers have recognised leadership and management responsibilities, it may be appropriate to agree objectives that focus on specific areas of this work, e.g. developing monitoring and evaluation expertise.

Figure 2.1: DfEE categories of objectives for teachers

Characteristics of effective objectives

Objective setting is intended to bring about change. Where objectives have been helpful to teachers they have generally obeyed the fundamental rules of clarity and precision, i.e. keeping them short and simple! Above all, objectives need to be:

- *consistent* with the values of the school and departmental objectives;
- *precise*: clear and well defined, using positive terminology;
- *challenging*: in order to stimulate high standards of performance and to encourage improvement;
- *measurable*: they can be related to quantified or qualitative performance measures;
- *achievable* within the capabilities of the individual and the constraints of resources;
- *agreed* by the team leader and the teacher, the aim being to provide for the ownership, not the imposition of objectives; and
- *time-related*: achievable within a defined time scale.

The **SMART** mnemonic, described in Figure 2.2 below, conveniently summarises the characteristics of effective objectives.

Principles of objective setting

Objectives should:

- be stated in clear, unambiguous language;
- be few in number (two to five) depending on their complexity;
- be measurable or observable;
- be challenging;
- be realistic and attainable;
- be job-orientated and related to improved competence;
- be related to, and consistent with, the philosophy of the school and the LEA;
- include an 'action plan' with steps for implementation;
- include some statement of what is considered to be an acceptable performance;
- be discussed at agreed intervals during the year by the parties concerned and modified if necessary; and
- be regularly and systematically monitored.

Following the agreement of objectives, the team leader has the important task of supporting the professional development of the teacher. Enquiring about progress and discussing issues as they arise

S = SPECIFIC	Objectives should be clear, unambiguous and understandable and should provide criteria for monitoring their progress. They should be expressed in terms of active verbs which focus attention on process, e.g. 'Undertake an audit which will aid review of the PSE policy by end of May' NOT 'hold discussions about the PSE provision in the school'.
M = MEASURABLE	Objectives not only enable progress to be monitored, they also provide criteria which enable us to evaluate the success of our achievement, e.g. quantity, quality, time, money. They are measures of success, e.g. 'Increase the percentage of parents attending school reporting evenings by 10 per cent' NOT 'improve parental support of the school'.
A = ACHIEVABLE	Objectives need to be achievable in terms of time and available resources, otherwise expectations will not be realised and commitment to future activities will be lost. However, they should be challenging yet within the reach of a competent and committed person. There is a temptation to set simple objectives which do not motivate because they are not demanding.
R = RELEVANT	Objectives should be relevant to the needs of the teacher as well as to the priorities of the school and the department so that the objective is aligned to school goals. The capabilities of individuals should enable progress to be made. If certain skills are lacking, programmes of training may need to be considered before a plan is implemented, e.g. 'Reorganise the classroom to aid small-group work' NOT 'plan how small group work could be improved'.
T = TIME-FRAMED	Without a time frame, targets provide no real criteria for monitoring progress. Each target should be linked to a short-term, mid-term or long-term reference point which will act as a marker and help to keep the implementation of a plan on course, e.g. 'Complete the audit by the end of autumn'.

Figure 2.2: SMART objectives

are just two ways in which this may be achieved. The team leader and teacher may also agree to approach other colleagues for support and advice in relation to any of the objectives.

Performance management objectives

Although the guidance offered in earlier sections can contribute to the process of writing SMART objectives, there is no ideal way of recording objectives. Schools will find it helpful to trial a variety of formats for recording objectives. However, uppermost in schools' minds should be the need to record objectives in such a way that teachers:

- understand precisely what is involved in achieving them;
- are appropriately positioned to achieve them;
- are clear about the steps they need to take to achieve them;
- know the timelines involved; and
- understand the criteria against which the objectives will be reviewed.

Some examples are set out below.

Examples: Professional development objectives

Here, the school has decided to adopt a format in which a global objective is agreed and an accompanying action plan then negotiated in order to meet SMART criteria. In this way, teachers know precisely what they need to do, by when, and with whose assistance; they can also monitor their success in working towards the objective with team leaders.

1. OBJECTIVE: To develop a resource of differentiated worksheets.

ACTION PLAN: Discuss with head of department by (specify date).

Discuss at department meeting (specify date).

Collate range of worksheets from colleagues by (specify date).

Produce and circulate catalogue index by (specify date).

Update catalogue twice per year.

Review contents of catalogue and usefulness to colleagues (specify date).

---

2. OBJECTIVE: Make greater use of group work in teaching GCSE syllabus.

ACTION PLAN: Look through scheme of work to identify appropriate topics for group work by (specify date).

Plan to use group work with both GCSE groups at least once each half-term (specify date).

Discuss pros and cons of such work with pupils (end of third and sixth sessions).

Review value of group work in terms of pupil enjoyment, motivation and understanding (end of third and sixth sessions).

3. OBJECTIVE: Increase use of computer network by groups in years 7 & 8

ACTION PLAN: Discuss possible use of computer software in context of Y7 & 8 syllabus with ICT coordinator by (specify date).

Discuss outcomes of discussions with ICT coordinator with HOD and department by (specify date).

Agree specific curriculum development target with HOD and department by (specify date).

Negotiate training in use of selected software with professional development coordinator by (specify date) and trial scheme of work by (specify date).

Discuss scheme of work developed with HOD and agree time for department training and implementation by (specify date).

Review success of development in terms of pupil interest and understanding and the reaction and comments of department staff by (specify date).

Examples: Pupil progress objectives

1. Aim for most (85%) of the class to be constructing basic essays demonstrating: a) both simple and complex sentence structure; b) correct paragraphing; c) a range of punctuation (including commas and apostrophes) usually used accurately; d) vocabulary choices are imaginative and used precisely, by the end of the year.*

2. To raise achievement of under-achieving ethnic minority groups in own history class by 2–3%.*

* Source : Performance Management in Schools, DfEE 2000a: 17

Examples: Leadership and management objectives

1. To improve the attendance of Year 9 pupils from 87 per cent to 90 per cent by the end of this academic year using the new electronic registration system.

2. To acquire the skills of lesson observation employed by members of the senior management team in order to monitor the quality of teaching and learning within the department prior to the introduction of the new teaching and learning policy next September.

3. To improve my skills when chairing meetings of the year team by:
   - attending a recommended course and applying the learning in context;
   - observing others with appropriate skills chairing meetings;
   - arranging for my team leader to observe me chairing meetings and to offer feedback.

Chapter 3

The performance management cycle: monitoring stage

Effective performance management requires the regular and systematic monitoring of progress and a commitment to ongoing support. A sizeable proportion of this monitoring and support activity will be self-managed, with teachers already using self- and/or department-initiated methods for monitoring progress. However, the team leader is responsible for monitoring the teacher's progress against the agreed objectives. During the 12–month cycle, an effective team leader can supplement the quality and challenge of this process in a variety of ways (see Figure 3.1).

Informal meetings and discussions	Formal meetings and discussions
• perhaps just a 'phone call' to keep in touch and provide support or coaching.	• which might result in objectives and implementation plans being modified because outside circumstances have changed.

Figure 3.1: Monitoring the achievement of objectives

Team leaders are likely to be able to base their monitoring activity on existing current practice. Examples might include:

- lesson observations;
- scrutiny of pupils' work;
- monitoring of weekly/termly plans; and
- monitoring test results/exam results.

Lesson observation

Lesson observation is an important means of gathering data for performance review purposes. If performance management is about raising the standard of pupil achievements by improving teacher effectiveness, then looking at what actually happens within teaching and learning contexts is vital. The major premise in carrying out lesson observation is that the:

- evaluation of lessons should lead to teachers becoming more effective; and
- outcomes of observation should enable clear objectives for improvement to be agreed.

The DfEE's performance management requirement is that teachers should normally be observed teaching on at least one occasion. Team leaders (reviewers) should have a clear understanding of the context in which an observed lesson is given. They will need to ensure that they are fully briefed by the teacher (reviewee) before the observation begins so that they are clear about the aims of the lesson, the profile of the group(s) being taught, the location of the lesson within a sequence, etc. Reviewers should also discuss their impressions of the lesson with the reviewee, a task they should normally aim to undertake within two working days of the observation.

A number of schools will have already used lesson observation for purposes other than performance management review and will have already appreciated its value, for example as part of wider monitoring and evaluation procedures, as preparation for external inspection. Teaching is far from being a routine activity and no single observation is likely to typify the generality of a teacher's classroom performance. Therefore, within the context of performance management review, lesson observation is only one of a number of available monitoring and data-gathering techniques.

Operational principles for lesson observation

Lesson observation should be carried out within a framework of agreed operational principles, such as those outlined below:

- the observation should be based on a mutual understanding between the reviewer and reviewee of the context, purpose, procedures, criteria and outcomes of the observation and especially of their potential to shed light on the success or otherwise with which the objectives are being met;
- both reviewer and reviewee should understand, and if necessary clarify, their respective responsibilities for acting upon the recommendations following an observation;
- the observation should be linked to a programme of professional support and development;
- the observation should be fair and equitable and should be seen to be so both in general and by respecting equal opportunities, particularly in relation to gender and race;
- the observation should be reasonably comprehensive, sampling an appropriate range of the teacher's classroom teaching;
- it should be valid and hence accurate and comprehensive in assessing teaching quality; and
- the lesson observation process should be practicable, avoid being too complex, bureaucratic and time consuming and, above all, lead to improvement.

However, observation continues to be a source of considerable anxiety for many teachers. Some of this anxiety is brought about by resentment that the autonomy of the teacher is being invaded. Another form of resentment stems from those who believe that observation of colleagues at work in the classroom has always taken place, albeit informally. There is little doubt that for many unused to regular or systematic observation since their early days in the profession, formalised and structured observation is a sensitive issue. So how can apprehension about the classroom observation process be limited? It is helpful for schools to develop a strategy that aims to:

- promote genuine discussion of teaching issues between teachers, perhaps through carrying out a whole-school review or constructing a school development plan;
- encourage teachers to observe other colleagues, possibly more experienced than themselves;
- encourage peer observation/feedback on specific and negotiated aspects of teaching (e.g. pupil involvement; on/off task behaviour; use of praise; use of question types);
- provide 'dry runs' of classroom observation – i.e. short observations carried out by those who will be involved in the process; and
- facilitate a self-observation exercise using audio and/or video recording.

Lesson observation is likely to be more effective in improving teaching if the focus of the observer is narrowed to certain specific features of a teacher's work in the classroom. A teacher's activities in the classroom are many and varied; if the observer attempts to observe all of these, little is likely to be gained and the result is likely to be some rather superficial observations. Data produced as a result of focused observations is likely to lead to more meaningful changes in working practice.

Observation inevitably involves making judgements; these must be made on the basis of agreed criteria and records should, where appropriate, note the observation that gave rise to the judgement. Without these criteria the observer is in danger of making arbitrary judgements, often looking at lessons in terms of how s/he would have taught them, or in being excessively critical of things recognised to be intrinsic faults. Feedback of descriptive rather than judgemental data is likely to lead to a far more productive process, with valuable information provided for discussion between observer and teacher at monitoring meetings.

During lesson observations, the observer should record the features of teaching which enable pupils to learn; if the converse is true, diagnose what is not working well enough and what could be done to improve matters. Evaluation and setting an agenda for development are starting points, but are of limited value unless monitoring is in place, carried out to agreed criteria and the outcomes discussed.

The reviewer should prepare for the lesson observation having:	The reviewee should prepare for the lesson observation having:
• prepared appropriately; • clearly understood the purpose and nature of the observation; • noted the date, time and location of the lesson observation; • reflected on the focus area(s) for the lesson observation; • considered a possible strategy for recording the findings of the lesson observation; • acquainted him/herself with the pro forma to be used for recording what is observed; • tried to ensure that his/her presence does not adversely affect the atmosphere of the lesson; • ensured that courtesies are observed; and • agreed the time and venue for feedback.	• prepared appropriately; • clarified the purpose, nature and content of the lesson, e.g. lesson plan, place of lesson in module/scheme; • communicated the nature of the teaching group, the planned use of resources, non-teaching staff, etc.; • ensured that courtesies are observed; • agreed the time and venue for feedback.

There are many ways of observing performance within the classroom. It is important that reviewers are aware of the various methods and the advantages and disadvantages of each. The type of classroom observation decided upon will depend on:

- the chosen focus of the lesson observation;
- the purpose of the observation; and
- the experience of the observer in carrying out the process.

The most commonly available recording methods at the disposal of the reviewer and reviewee are summarised in Figure 3.1.

Successful lesson observation can provide a valuable starting point for the professional discussion on which the performance review is based. However, sufficient time should be allowed for both the reviewer and the reviewee to reflect upon the information gathered and the way in which it may relate to the objectives set at the review meeting.

The DfEE's suggested format for a standard pro forma for recording observations together with appropriate guidance can be found in the *Model Performance Management Policy* (DfEE 2000b: 18–21). It may be the case that some pro formas are more suited to particular observations but whatever pro formas are used, it is essential that commonly understood and agreed criteria for teaching and learning are agreed upon. A range of documents has been written to define clearly the characteristics of effective teaching and learning, e.g. the Hay McBer research (Hay McBer 2000) and OFSTED's guidance found in the Handbooks for Inspection. These handbooks also remind us that some observations may focus on *one* aspect of teaching and emphasise the point that the overriding consideration for evaluating the quality of teaching is how well pupils learn.

• **Open recording**	Observer uses blank sheet of paper and either notes down key points in the lesson, or uses a form of shorthand/longhand and writes quickly to record what happens.
• **Tally systems**	Observer puts down a tally or tick every time particular events occur against predetermined criteria agreed between reviewer and reviewee, e.g. every time a teacher gives praise or asks a closed question. The result is factual rather than judgemental. The aim is to produce a pattern of classroom events.
• **Timed systems**	Observer scans the classroom at predetermined intervals, e.g every two minutes, and either writes down what is happening or puts a mark under one of the series of predetermined categories which describe possible classroom events. Again, this shows a pattern of events and the record is factual.
• **Prompting questions**	Observer is asked to provide answers to a series of questions about classroom work. Prompting questions can cast the observer in a judgemental role, encouraging him/her to impose personal views. This can be prevented if the questions are designed to elicit factual and objective answers rather than opinions.
• **Diagram**	Observer records what happens on a diagram of the classroom. This can be factual and descriptive.
• **Audio/Audio-visual recording methods**	These can be used on their own or in conjunction with written methods of recording. They are selective depending on the position of microphones and cameras. They enable the reviewer and reviewee to replay the lesson during a feedback discussion.

Figure 3.1: Methods for recording lesson observation

EXAMPLE 7: LESSON OBSERVATION PRO FORMA

Teacher: _____ Team leader: _____

Date: _____ Class/Group: _____ Age range: _____

Lesson/Activity: _____

Are the aims and objectives of the lesson/activity made clear to the class/group?

Have these aims and objectives been translated into activities which illustrate a planned progression of knowledge, skills and understanding?

Is there evidence of long- and short-term curriculum or lesson planning for this group?

What did the pupils do?

What did the pupils learn?

Were the pupils challenged by the work? Was the range of work suitable for the age and ability of the pupils?

Did the pupils enjoy the lesson? Were they appropriately involved in the lesson?

Are clear assessment criteria available for this work? Was the assessment carried out satisfactorily?

General comment on the lesson – strengths and weaknesses.

Suggestions for future lessons.

EXAMPLE 8: LESSON OBSERVATION PRO FORMA	Yes	No
Teacher planning		
a) Objectives are communicated clearly at the start of the lesson.		
b) Materials are ready.		
c) There is a good structure to the lesson.		
d) The lesson is reviewed at the end.		
e) The learning of all pupils is incorporated within the teacher's planning.		
Subject knowledge and understanding		
a) Teacher has a thorough knowledge of the subject content covered in the lesson.		
b) Subject material was appropriate for the lesson.		
c) Knowledge is made relevant and interesting for pupils.		
Teaching methods		
a) The lesson is linked to previous teaching or learning.		
b) The ideas and experiences of pupils are drawn upon.		
c) A variety of activities and questioning techniques is used.		
d) Instructions and explanations are clear and specific.		
e) The teacher involves all pupils, listens to them and responds appropriately.		
f) Appropriate methods of differentiation are used.		
Pupil management		
a) Pupils are praised regularly for their good effort and achievement.		
b) Prompt action is taken to address poor behaviour.		
c) All pupils are treated fairly, with an equal emphasis on the work of boys and girls, and all ability groups.		
Pupil assessment		
a) Pupil understanding is assessed throughout the lesson by the use of teacher's questions.		
b) Mistakes and misconceptions are utilised by the teacher and used constructively to facilitate learning.		
c) Pupils' written work is assessed regularly and accurately.		

Pupil outcomes	Yes	No
a) Pupils remain fully engaged throughout the lesson and make progress in the lesson.		
b Pupils understand what work is expected of them during the lesson.		
c) The pupil outcomes of the lesson are consistent with the objectives set at the beginning.		
d) The teacher and pupils work at a good pace.		
Use of time and resources		
a) Time is well used and the learning is maintained for the full time available.		
b) A good pace is maintained throughout the lesson.		
c) Good use is made of any support available.		
d) Appropriate learning resources are used, e.g. ICT.		
Homework		
a) Homework is set if appropriate.		
b) The learning objectives are explicit and relate to the work in progress.		
c) Homework is followed up if it has been set previously.		

Strengths

Areas for development

Feedback

The main aim of gathering data from lesson observation must be to influence the effectiveness of the teachers' performance. Therefore, the most important rule in giving feedback is to focus on the teaching and learning that has taken place. Discussion of the data by the observer and the teacher during the monitoring stage should lead to valuable learning. However, this will only be true if the atmosphere is positive and supportive and based on the mutual trust established between the reviewer and reviewee at the planning stage. Feedback normally works best if it is:

- given within 48 hours of the observation;
- based on careful and systematic recording;
- based on data which is factual;
- interpreted with reference to known and agreed criteria;
- given as part of a two-way discussion; and
- the basis for future development strategies.

In giving feedback on the teaching and learning that has been observed, the reviewer should:

- focus on the *evidence* that has been recorded rather than on impressions gained;
- focus on *description* rather than on judgement, i.e. illustrate with specific and practical examples from the observation;
- focus on *sharing* ideas rather than on giving evidence;
- focus on the *needs of the reviewee* rather than on those of the reviewer;
- focus on *what the reviewee can use* rather than on what the reviewer might like to give;
- focus on *what* is observed rather than on *why* something might have happened;
- allow the teacher *time to reflect and comment* in order to emphasise the dialogue that is taking place;
- be *positive.*

The reviewer should prepare to give feedback having:	The reviewee should prepare for the feedback by:
• identified desired outcomes following the feedback; • thought about ways to feed back findings; • considered how to initiate the discussion and how to invite contributions from the teacher; • decided what to draw particular attention to and how to do this; • ensured a relaxed but professional atmosphere; • formed clear, accurate judgements, based on evidence; • recognised strengths as well as areas for development; • focused on teaching, not the teacher • included the views of the teacher • given helpful advice which will lead to action • agreed and recorded any action to be taken	• agreeing time and venue for feedback • agreeing and recording any action to be taken.

Chapter 4

The performance management cycle: review stage

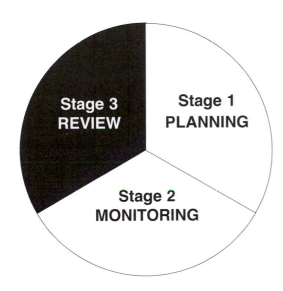

The third and final stage of the performance management cycle is the annual review of the teacher's performance. The team leader and the teacher will use the objectives recorded at the planning meeting (Stage 1) as a focus for discussions on the teacher's achievements. The review will also serve as an opportunity to identify and respond to development needs. The annual review will be combined with agreeing objectives for the following performance management cycle. The review discussion should provide an opportunity for genuine dialogue and involve:

The review meeting

- further consideration, if necessary, of the job description;
- review of the teacher's work, including successes and areas for development identified since the planning and setting objectives;
- discussion of professional development needs;
- discussion of career development, if applicable;
- discussion of the teacher's contribution to the policies and management of the school, and any constraints which the circumstances of the school place on him or her;

- identification of objectives for future action and development; and
- clarification of the points to be included in the review statement.

Review meetings are most likely to be successful when a series of factors are present and when some others are eliminated or reduced in terms of their influence. Figure 4.1 summarises these facilitating and hindering factors:

Factors likely to promote successful review meetings	Factors likely to mitigate against successful review meetings
• adequate preparation by both parties; • a clearly agreed agenda; • sharing of relevant data and documentation; • adequate time; • a limit on the number of reviews undertaken by a team leader; • prompt write-up of the review statement; • effective interpersonal skills; • positive nature of previous relationships between the team leader and the teacher; • all parties giving the review high priority; and • no interruptions.	• inadequate time; • low priority given to the review; • sudden changes in planned programme; • a lack of preparation by either or both parties; • not keeping to the agenda; • interruptions; and • poor prior relationships.

Figure 4.1: Factors affecting the success of review meetings

A great deal of the success of the review meeting will depend on the quality of preparation by both the team leader and the teacher. Preparation for the meeting should be thorough if the team leader and the teacher are going to have an informed, professional discussion. Figure 4.2 highlights the basic preparation necessary on the part of team leaders and teachers to ensure a satisfactory review meeting.

The reviewer should come to the meeting:	The reviewee should come to the meeting:
• having discussed the time and venue for the meeting with the teacher; • having considered the teacher's job description; • with a copy of the school's agreed policy; • having considered possible areas for discussion – an agenda; • having prepared a strategy for structuring the discussion according to the agreed agenda; • being prepared to listen actively to the teacher's views and suggestions; • being prepared to help the reviewee to clarify the nature and meaning of the review focus; • having thought of possible professional development needs and activities; • with the aim of encouraging the teacher to talk constructively about key areas and of ensuring that the discussions are positive; and • with the aim of keeping the discussion focused on the agreed scope of the review.	• having prepared by reflecting on the agreed scope of the review, the job description, the lesson observation, other supporting information and the agreed agenda; • having reflected on a possible focus for the review meeting (a self-review exercise is useful preparation); • willing to discuss performance frankly and honestly; and • having thought of professional development needs and activities.

Figure 4.2: Preparation for the review meeting

During the review meeting the teacher should be encouraged to discuss those aspects of the job that have given him/her most satisfaction, as well as those areas they wish to develop further or in which they feel that they need support. If appropriate, the team leader should attempt to advise the teacher on how his/her strengths and talents might be used within the wider school context and also what support might be given to developing their professional expertise in other areas. The success of the review meeting relies very much upon the ability of the team leader to utilise the potential of the process to bring about a meaningful dialogue. The team leader's all-round skills and preparation are vital to the success of the process.

Reviewing skills

This section considers the nature and scope of the skills needed by team leaders and teachers when conducting a successful review meeting. However, it should be pointed out that these same skills are highly pertinent throughout each of the stages that comprise the performance management process. The skills required of the team leader to bring about a successful review process are summarised in Figure 4.3.

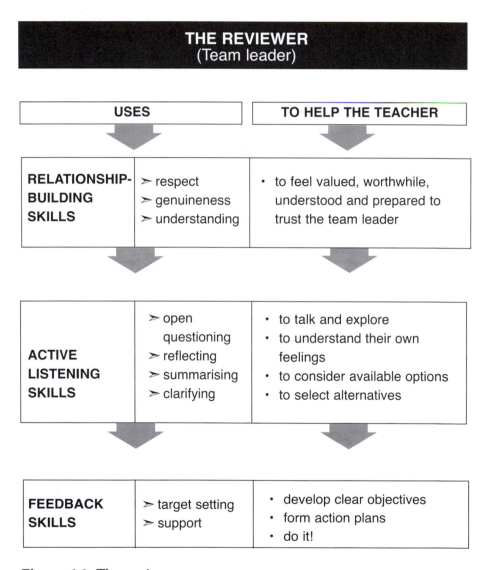

	THE REVIEWER (Team leader)	
	USES	**TO HELP THE TEACHER**
RELATIONSHIP-BUILDING SKILLS	➤ respect ➤ genuineness ➤ understanding	• to feel valued, worthwhile, understood and prepared to trust the team leader
ACTIVE LISTENING SKILLS	➤ open questioning ➤ reflecting ➤ summarising ➤ clarifying	• to talk and explore • to understand their own feelings • to consider available options • to select alternatives
FEEDBACK SKILLS	➤ target setting ➤ support	• develop clear objectives • form action plans • do it!

Figure 4.3: The review process

Relationship-building skills

Building and maintaining a productive relationship is the first important task of the team leader. By demonstrating respect, genuineness and understanding, the team leader encourages the teacher to feel valued and understood, thus leading to a trusting relationship. Through their behaviour, team leaders indicate to teachers that they are worthwhile, valuable and unique. Genuineness involves team leaders being 'themselves'; they need to be real, trustworthy and appropriately open about themselves. Empathising and understanding involves demonstrating the capacity to take the teacher's perspective on his or her professional context. Moreover, the challenge for team leaders is to achieve empathy without becoming so intimately involved that personal feelings mask or distort the teacher's view. Among the ways that team leaders can demonstrate these skills are the following:

- being punctual for meetings;
- being prepared;
- showing respect; and
- not being judgemental.

Active listening skills

Effective listening is an active skill. It involves not only hearing what is being said, but also judging what is meant by the words and the gestures used. During review discussions, reviewees may demonstrate some reluctance to express their fears and problems; they may be anxious about being criticised or judged. By listening actively the reviewer shows genuine interest and understanding and so is able to help the teacher to talk about and explore aspects of their work, understand their own feelings about pupil progress or pupils' behaviour, consider available options for bringing about changes and, finally, selecting alternatives which usually translate into future objectives. Active listening involves:

- sitting comfortably and trying to relax;
- making appropriate eye contact with the teacher;
- concentrating hard on what is said;
- trying not to interrupt;
- not letting personal concerns or biases get in the way of what is being said;
- using short nods to show that listening is taking place;
- picking up non-verbal communication – facial expressions, body posture, etc.;
- listening for verbal cues – hesitancy, rapid speech, tone of voice, etc.

Questioning

Good questioning skills are as essential as good listening skills. It is helpful to use different types of questions to encourage reviewees to offer relevant information about their classroom practice and development issues. Useful types of question are shown below.

Open questions	Open questions are intended to stimulate discussion, and encourage reviewees to disclose relevant information so that the team leader can pick up key words and probe for detail. A simple definition of an open question is one to which you cannot answer 'yes' or 'no'. These usually start with 'How', 'Which', 'What', 'Who', 'Why' and 'Where'. Example: 'Which of your objectives have brought about the greatest gains in pupil progress?' … 'Why is that, do you think?' … 'What do you think caused the problem?'
Follow-up questions	These questions enable the reviewer to follow up key words in order to gather more information. Example: 'If you had to identify the difficulties about achieving that objective, what would they be?'
Reflective questions	Reflective questions are those that allow the team leader to check his/her understanding of what the reviewee has said. They are questions that reflect, or repeat back to the teacher what has been said. In this way, it is possible to reflect both information and feelings. Example: 'Can I just check with you that what you did to overcome the major difficulty was …?'
Link questions	This is a useful technique for the team leader to use when attempting to move on to another topic or checking on a comment or something that was said earlier. Example: 'If I remember, you said … now you say … perhaps you can explain the difference?'

Final question	Even if the discussion is completed from the team leader's point of view, the reviewee may still have an issue he/she wants to raise. Example: 'Is there anything we have not covered, that you would like to raise?'

In the same way that some styles of questioning are likely to be supportive of the review process, certain other styles of questioning should be avoided because of their inhibiting effect on the process. The following categories of questions are unlikely to stimulate conversation or encourage open discussion:

Closed questions	Unlike open questions, closed questions are those that invite 'yes' or 'no' responses. They can be used occasionally to check facts but, when used too frequently, can make the discussion take the form of an interrogation. Example: 'Did you meet the deadline on Y2 reports?'
Value questions	These questions suggest that the team leader is looking for a certain answer based on his/her personal values. Such questions put teachers in the awkward position of not knowing whether to give their personal view or the one they feel the reviewer wants to hear. Example: 'You liked being involved with that project didn't you?'
Multiple questions	Asking more than one question at a time can confuse reviewees because they do not know which one to answer. Example: 'Why do you think this has happened and how do you think you responded to the criticism?'

Summarising

When summarising, the team leader attempts to condense and crystallise the fundamental nature of what is being said. Summarising is important and helpful to both team leader and reviewees because:

- the team leader can check that the reviewee has understood what has been said;
- it identifies the main points of the earlier discussion;
- it can encourage the teacher to elaborate further on the points summarised;
- it helps prevent the review from degenerating into a meaningless chat; and
- it helps the teacher recall what has been said.

In order to summarise, the team leader will probably need to make some notes. However, this note taking should not be allowed to distract from the process.

Clarifying

Effective review meetings will generate a vast range of information. Clarification can help to highlight significant points raised by the teacher in the course of the discussion. Done with care, team leaders make use of clarification to gain a true and accurate view of what is being conveyed by the teacher.

Reflecting

Reflecting is a powerful skill available to team leaders to help them recognise what is said by reviewees. Team leaders may be reflecting feelings, experience and content at any point in the review meeting. This is most successfully achieved when team leaders show attention not only to *what* is being said (content), but also to *how* it is being conveyed (feelings) possibly through non-verbal behaviour.

Feedback skills

People are motivated when their contribution is recognised and acknowledged. Consequently, giving praise is the most powerful element of feedback. Constructive feedback, when honest, specific and genuine, can increase self-awareness, offer options and encourage development. The following guidelines may be helpful here:

Start with the positive aspects

Colleagues are likely to want encouragement and to be told when they are doing something well. It can really help the teacher personally, as well as the tone of the discussion, to hear first about those aspects of the work that have been done well. For example: 'I really liked the way you dealt with the issues your Year 11 group raised.'

Be specific
Comments which are too general or superficial are unlikely to be useful to the teacher when it comes to developing his/her skills. Specific feedback offers more opportunity for personal learning. Relate feedback to specific items of behaviour. For example: 'You created a good atmosphere using that video clip and the role-play activity.'

Refer to behaviour which can be changed
It is not likely to be helpful to offer a colleague feedback about something over which they have no choice or influence. For example: 'If you were about four or five inches taller you probably wouldn't have control problems with that class.'

Offer alternatives
In the case of negative feedback in particular, it is crucial that the reviewee is offered alternative strategies for dealing with the problem. Offering ways in which the person could have done things differently – or turning the negative into a positive approach – is vital. For example: '... have you thought of trying ...?', '... might it be worthwhile ...?'

Be descriptive rather than evaluative
Telling a colleague what has been observed or heard and the effect that the action has had is likely to be of more benefit than merely saying that something was 'good', 'bad' or 'OK'. For example: 'Your tone of voice as you said that really made me feel that you were concerned.'

Feedback is likely to say as much about the giver as the receiver. It will communicate a good deal about your values and what we focus on in others.

Giving criticism

To bring about an improvement in performance it will be necessary, at times, to offer constructive criticism. The important thing for the reviewer is to do so without causing distress or resentment. The following guidelines may be helpful:

- introduce the issue directly;
- state the problem specifically;
- quote examples;
- invite an explanation;

- encourage the teacher to find solutions to the problem;
- state the agreed solution; and
- offer clear support to enable the teacher to act on the agreed solution.

For those on the receiving end of feedback it may be useful to consider the following points:

Listen to the feedback rather than immediately rejecting or arguing with it

Feedback can be uncomfortable, particularly when not expected; and yet it is feedback, conveyed sincerely and genuinely, that holds the greatest potential for bringing about improvements. Before dismissing such feedback it is important to remember that the perceptions that others have of our behaviour can be useful to us.

Be clear about what is being said

It is easy to jump to conclusions or to become immediately defensive when being given feedback. Make sure that the feedback is understood before any response is given. A useful way of dealing with this is to check for understanding by paraphrasing or repeating the criticism.

Check it out with others rather than relying on only one source

A second opinion might, in fact, tell you the extent to which a particular view is held by others. An isolated opinion may help you keep the feedback in perspective.

Meeting teachers' professional development needs

Teachers' professional development should focus on raising standards in the classroom, and therefore take account of objectives that enhance pupil learning as well as broader professional skills. Teachers should be encouraged to take ownership and give high priority to professional development. Schools and teachers should share responsibility and commitment for development. Professional development should:

- be in the context of continuing professional development;
- enable the teacher to improve their professional practice;
- stem from the teacher's performance review;
- be linked to school priorities as identified in the school development plan;
- be linked to the teacher's career aspirations (where applicable).

The professional needs of the teacher, as identified through the performance review process, may be met in a variety of ways:

Using in-house expertise	Team leaders or members of the senior management team might lead short courses on a range of skills, e.g. time management, interviewing, effective questioning, giving feedback, effective listening, negotiating, managing budgets, chairing meetings, etc.
Shadowing	Prospective team leaders/senior managers might shadow a more experienced colleague.
Joint lesson observation	The constituents of effective practice in teaching and learning might be discussed and views shared. This might lead to modelling of lessons.
Mentoring	Acting as mentor to a newly qualified teacher, or an ITT trainee, or a newly appointed team leader can be a very powerful professional development tool but care must be taken to ensure that the potential mentor has the appropriate skills to undertake such a role.
Successor training	Key posts within a school should have a potential successor in case of absence. The coaching of appropriate colleagues for such roles can be an effective route towards staff development.
Working groups	Leading or participating in groups when established to develop whole-school policies, or to undertake research on behalf of the school where improved or new practice is being sought.
Cascading	As a consequence of attending externally run courses all participants are expected to give feedback to relevant staff groups.
Tasked writing groups	These groups could be established to undertake research on behalf of the school in an area where improved practice is sought.

Application to external courses	Attendees should provide feedback to other colleagues as a part of normal practice.
Cluster training	Partnerships among schools can combine resources that bring in proven and talented trainers.
Network meetings	Networks are normally organised on a local basis to bring together functional groups, e.g. deputy head teachers, team leaders and subject specialists who can share good practice and visit each other's work place.
Professional associations/ General Teaching Council	These organise and run a range of professional development opportunities which add to networking potential.

Individual development planning

The emphasis of this book is on the potential of performance management to improve the performance of teachers. This vital developmental aspect occupies each element of the performance management cycle: planning, monitoring and review. Optimum benefit is more likely to be gained within a framework of personal development facilitated by individual development plans. Individual development planning is carried out by teachers, ideally with guidance, encouragement and help from their team leaders and others.

A teacher's individual development plan results from identifying the need for skills, knowledge and competence and defines the appropriate development to meet those perceived needs. Individual development plans can be created as an important outcome of a performance review and planning meeting. The four stages involved in preparing an individual development plan are shown in Figure 4.4.

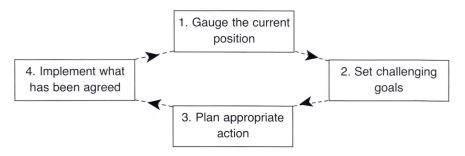

Figure 4.4: Stages in the individual development planning process

Examples of Individual Development Plans

EXAMPLE 1: PERSONAL IMPROVEMENT PLAN		
Please note under the following headings your objectives with some indication as to when you think these objectives may be realised.		
AREAS OF RESPONSIBILITY, e.g.	PERSONAL IMPROVEMENT OBJECTIVE(S)	TO BE ACHIEVED BY
THE COMMUNITY		
THE CURRICULUM		
LEA & GOVERNORS		

MONITORING & EVALUATION PUPILS		
RESOURCES		
STAFF		
OTHERS		

EXAMPLE 2: PERSONAL ACTION PLAN

INITIATIVES:

1. ACTIONS BY ME:

2. ACTIONS BY MY COLLEGE/SCHOOL/LEA/OTHER ON MY RECOMMENDATION

3. STRATEGIES TO BE USED IN FURTHERANCE OF INITIATIVES (1) & (2)

4. LIAISON TO BE STRENGTHENED WITH:

5. STRATEGIES TO BE USED IN FURTHERANCE OF (4)

6. OTHER ACTIONS/INTENTIONS

7. SUPPORT NETWORKS TO BE USED

8. CONTINUING PROFESSIONAL DEVELOPMENT TO BE ARRANGED FOR ME

FOR COLLEAGUES

9. DETAILED TIMETABLE

Action to be taken by the end of the month

By the end of the term

By the end of the academic year

10. NAME OF THE APPRAISER WHO IS PREPARED TO ASSIST ME IN (A) PREPARATION AND (B) IMPLEMENTATION OF THE ACTION PLAN

NAME(S)

Signed: Date:

Within 10 days of the review meeting, the team leader will prepare a written review statement recording the main points made at the review and the conclusions reached, including any identified development needs and activities recorded in a separate annex (but forming part of) the review statement. Once written, the team leader will give the teacher a copy of the statement. The teacher may within 10 days of first having access to the statement, add to it comments in writing.

(Model Performance Management Policy, DfEE 2000b: 6)

It is advisable that the review statement is written as soon as possible after the review, while the facts remain fresh in the team leader's memory. The DfEE requires the statement to have been written within ten working days of the review meeting. Following the review meeting, the team leader will need to prepare a written review statement summarising the main points made and the conclusions reached, including an assessment of how well the objectives agreed at the planning stage (Stage 1) have been met. Development needs and activities should be recorded in a separate annex, which will form a part of the review statement. Having received a copy of the statement from the team leader, the teacher has a further ten working days within which to add to it comments in writing and sign.

In its *Model Performance Management Policy* (DfEE 2000b), the DfEE proposes a set of pro forma for use by schools.

Both the teacher's individual plan and the review statement are personal and confidential documents. The headteacher should keep review statements for at least three years. The DfEE requirement is that there will be two copies of the review statement:

one held by the teacher and another held by the head on a central file, to which the team leader or Governors responsible for making decisions regarding pay could request access. A copy of the heads' review statement should go to the Chair of Governors.

(Model Performance Management Policy, DfEE 2000b: 6)

Other action in relation to review outcomes include:

Action	Responsibility
• Reflect individual training and development needs in the development plan and in the school's programme for professional development.	Head teacher
• Hand training and development needs recorded in the review statement to member of staff responsible for these areas within the school.	Head teacher
• Report to the governing body annually on the effectiveness of the procedures and the training and development needs of staff.	Head teacher
• Provide chief education officer, on request, a summary of the performance assessment section of the head's review statement.	Chair of Governors

Complaints about the performance review statement

If a complaint is made about the performance review statement, the review officer is responsible for reviewing the complaint. In the case of a teacher's complaint, the review officer is the head teacher as long as the head teacher is not the teacher's team leader. Should this be the case, the head teacher should arrange for another head teacher to be the review officer.

Where a complaint is made by the head teacher about his or her review statement, the review officer should be the chair of governors or his/her representatives from the governing body.

Chapter 5

Coordinating, monitoring and evaluating the school's arrangements for performance management

For something as sensitive as performance management, there are rarely quick-fix solutions. The process often fails because it is difficult to coordinate its many facets. It takes time and continuous effort to implement and then maintain the process and ensure that everyone is committed to its principles and practices them. Effective coordination, then, is vital since the process needs to be embedded in:

- a thorough understanding of the school's current position and in its vision for future development;
- a complete awareness of the school's culture, context and unique characteristics;
- a set of principles that are pertinent to the school's needs and are acceptable to all staff;
- an understanding of the integral nature of performance management in associated management processes;
- an evident commitment from senior managers of the school;
- arrangements that are straightforward, socially acceptable; and
- a development culture rather than an accountability culture.

A vital aspect of the school's coordination of performance management will be to maintain high and consistent standards throughout. To do this, schools will need to ensure thorough training for team leaders and teachers in the skills required to operate their performance management arrangements. Whereas many among the staff will already have the skills of objective setting, feedback giving and coaching, they may not have been consciously practised with peers. Schools should not make the mistake of restricting training to team leaders; teachers also need to know the part they might play in maximising the opportunities presented by the process. In particular, schools should aim to ensure that:

Coordination

- top-up training is made available for all staff to ensure that the principles and practices associated with performance management are sustained;
- training in performance management is available for all new staff joining the school;
- the skills levels of team leaders are maintained and enhanced; and
- team leaders are offered workshops where they can share their experiences and seek support.

The person appointed to coordinate the implementation and ongoing management of the school's arrangements is likely to be a member of the senior management team/leadership group. He/she will need relevant skills and experience of staff development and, perhaps more importantly, the confidence of teachers within the school. Among the coordinator's responsibilities are the following:

- supporting team leaders and ensuring that they receive adequate briefing and training;
- briefing all staff on the school's arrangements for performance management;
- organising the timetabling and administration of the process;
- implementing and maintaining procedures which link training and development opportunities with outcomes; and
- ensuring that the school's procedures are regularly and systematically monitored and evaluated.

Monitoring and evaluation

It is clearly important to monitor the introduction of performance management with care, but it is equally vital to continue to monitor and evaluate the school's arrangements regularly and systematically beyond that initial period. In this context, monitoring refers to those processes involved in the collection of data and information, while evaluation describes the ordering and presentation of data and the judgements made subsequently. Both processes are complementary and, in relation to the school's performance management arrangements, should help:

- inform future decision making;
- improve operational efficiency;
- optimise available resources;
- highlight future resource requirements;
- identify strengths and weaknesses;
- clarify aims, objectives and priorities; and
- raise the quality of learning and teaching.

It is convenient to think of the monitoring and evaluation of performance management as a cyclical process. Having established the values and the aims of the school-based process, it becomes necessary to monitor the process's separate but interrelated components and activities. Data gathered in this way can then be used to evaluate not only the effectiveness but also the efficiency of the process. Evaluation outcomes should guide any action required to bring about improvements. Figure 5.1 sets out the key elements of the monitoring and evaluation of the performance review process in schools.

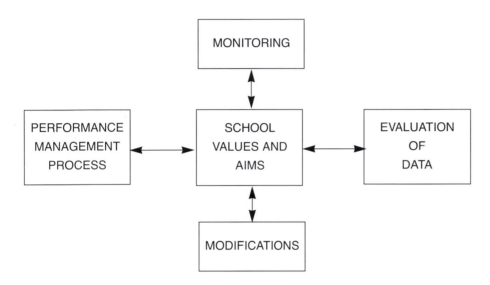

Figure 5.1: Monitoring and evaluation of the performance management process

The most effective and efficient method of monitoring and evaluating how well performance management is working is to ask those most acutely involved – senior managers, individual teachers and team leaders. The ultimate test, of course, is analysing school performance data in order to establish the extent to which improvements can be attributed to performance management. It may be difficult to establish a direct connection, but more detailed discussion and probing with team leaders, teachers and senior managers on the impact of the process may reveal specific areas in which performance has been improved, which could be linked to an overall performance measure.

EVALUATION SCHEDULE 1: PERFORMANCE MANAGEMENT POLICY

- Does the school have a written performance management policy?

- Does the policy clearly distinguish between sections that are based on the performance regulations and those that are included by the school?

- In what ways have the staff been involved in its development?

- Has the policy been agreed by the governing body?

- Do the staff know how performance management works?

- How have staff been made aware of their responsibilities and rights within it?

- Have the potential benefits of performance management been made clear to staff?

- Is the policy fair?

- Are all teachers treated consistently?

- Are the school's performance management arrangements simple to operate and implement?

- Does the policy encourage teachers to share good practice and to build up a shared understanding of effective teaching skills?

EVALUATION SCHEDULE 2: PERFORMANCE MANAGEMENT CYCLE

- Has the precise timing of the performance management cycle been agreed?

- Does the cycle fit well with the school's other planning arrangements?

- Are staff aware of the intention behind each of the three stages of the cycle?

EVALUATION SCHEDULE 3: PLANNING STAGE

- Is the team leader's role clearly defined?

- Has each teacher and team leader agreed what should be the focus of the teacher's work at the start of the review cycle?

- Are clear job descriptions in place?

- Does the planning stage offer adequate opportunity to discuss teachers' priorities, the needs of pupils and specific objectives for the forthcoming year?

- Is the discussion focused on the progress made by pupils and the teacher's role in this?

- Is the school development pan used effectively to provide background information about the prior attainment of the pupils?

- How effectively have objectives been agreed and individual plans completed?

EVALUATION SCHEDULE 4: OBJECTIVES

- Are objectives agreed in the key areas of pupil progress and developing and improving teachers' professional practice?

- Are the agreed objectives clear, concise, challenging, flexible and measurable?

- Are the numbers of agreed objectives appropriate for each teacher?

- Do teachers understand what their objectives involve and how they will be reviewed?

- Do teachers' objectives relate to the objectives in the school development plan?

- Is a teacher's individual plan agreed with the team leader where responsibilities and objectives are clearly stated?

EVALUATION SCHEDULE 5: MONITORING STAGE
• Do team leaders pay continuous attention to teachers' progress during the year?
• What methods are used to monitor such progress?
• Is the individual plan for each teacher completed and kept up to date?
• Is the process of classroom observation set out clearly?
• How effective is the pro forma for the purpose of recording?
• Have observers and teachers received adequate preparation and training for undertaking lesson observation?
• Are focus areas agreed in preparation for the observation?
• What steps are taken to ensure that the observed lesson proceeds in as normal a way as possible?
• Is full and constructive feedback offered to each teacher within an appropriate interval of the lesson?

EVALUATION SCHEDULE 6: REVIEW MEETING

• Does the review provide an opportunity for teacher and team leader to reflect on the teacher's performance in a structured way?

• Is the opportunity adequate for recognising achievements and for discussing areas for improvement and professional development?

• Is the focus of the review firmly on how to raise performance and improve effectiveness?

• Has the team leader made a professional judgement about the overall effectiveness of the teacher with the individual objectives as a focus?

• Does this judgement take account of the stage the teacher is at in his/her career?

• Are the outcomes of the review meeting recorded appropriately in the review statement?

• Is the review statement written within the 10 days allowed?

EVALUATION SCHEDULE 7: ROLES AND RESPONSIBILITIES

- How effectively does the head teacher implement the school's performance management policy?

- Are all required performance management reviews taking place?

- Has the head teacher ensured that team leaders carry out their responsibilities effectively?

- Has the head teacher ensured that individual plans and standards are agreed for all teachers and that professional development is targeted?

- Has the head teacher ensured that monitoring of teaching is taking place and that feedback allows the teacher to reflect on his/her performance?

- How effective is the governing body in fulfilling its strategic role?

EVALUATION SCHEDULE 8: EQUAL OPPORTUNITIES

- What steps are taken to ensure fairness and consistency of judgement within the system?

- How does the school ensure that all teachers have equality of opportunity to achieve their full potential and are not discriminated against when agreeing objectives and assessing performance?

- How does the school ensure that teachers are not discriminated against because of age, disability, gender, nationality, race, religion, or are treated unfairly because they work part time or are union representatives?

- Does the school make every attempt to avoid assumptions about individuals based on stereotypes?

EVALUATION SCHEDULE 9: REVIEW STATEMENT

- When will the review statement be written?

- Is there an agreed school format for the review statement?

- How well have the review statements been completed?

EVALUATION SCHEDULE 10: DOCUMENTATION

- Is the performance management policy in place?

- What written guidelines are required to support the process?

- What pro forma need to be produced to support the process?

- How successful have we been in avoiding over-elaborate forms and a scheme that is largely a form-filling exercise?

EVALUATION SCHEDULE 11: REVIEW SKILLS

- Are team leaders providing good feedback throughout the year as well as during formal review meetings?

- How effective are both team leaders and teachers in their preparation for performance review meetings?

- How well are team leaders conducting such meetings with particular reference to:

  - creating the right atmosphere;

  - working to a clear structure;

  - using praise to get people to relax, and to motivate and provide them with encouragement;

  - letting the individual do most of the talking;

  - inviting self-appraisal;

  - discussing performance, not personality;

  - being positive;

  - not springing surprises on the individuals; and

  - agreeing realistic and measurable objectives and an individual plan of action.

- How effective has performance management been in developing teachers' skills and capabilities?

- How well have team leaders carried out their roles as coach, mentor and counsellor?

References

DfEE (1998) *Teachers: Meeting the Challenge of Change.* Government Green Paper.

DfEE (2000a) *Performance Management in Schools: Performance Management Framework.* Ref DfEE 0051/2000. April 2000.

DfEE (2000b) *Performance Management in Schools: Model Performance Management Policy.*

Hay McBer (2000) *Research into Teacher Effectiveness: A Model of Teacher Effectiveness.* Report to the DfEE. June 2000.

Index